my wins JOURNAL

write or doodle and celebrate YOU

These wins belong to:

_____

WHAT ARE WINS?

A win is something you did that makes you proud of yourself. It can be big or it can be small. A win could be "I scored a goal today at my soccer game!" It could also be "I focused for five minutes on my homework." Or "I helped an adult take out the trash." Or even "I helped someone instead of yelling at them." The more wins you celebrate, the more wins you will see. They will keep building and growing like a snowball.

HOW TO USE THIS JOURNAL

Whenever you do something that you are proud of, write or draw it here in this journal. Keep track of all your wins and watch them as they pile up.

Celebrate yourself!

what is a LANGUAGE NINJA?

Someone who is skilled at using their words to empower themself.

Qualities of a Language Ninja

- respectful
- brave
- self-controlled
- kind
- change-maker
- peaceful
- playful
- creative

List your Language Ninja qualities:

Draw yourself as a Language Ninja

What wins are you celebrating today?
write or doodle and celebrate YOU

my wins inspire

WITH MY WORDS I CREATE!

What wins are you celebrating today?
write or doodle and celebrate YOU

my words create change

Let's check in!

Take a look at the wins you have written. What do you notice?

_____
_____
_____
_____
_____
_____
_____
_____

Write your affirmations:

I can: _____

I will: _____

I am: _____

Draw what makes you proud!

What wins are you celebrating today?
write or doodle and celebrate YOU

I AM PLAYFUL

What wins are you celebrating today?

write or doodle and celebrate YOU

Let's check in!

Take a look at the wins you have written. What do you notice?

_____
_____
_____
_____
_____
_____
_____
_____

Write your affirmations:

I can: _____
I will: _____
I am: _____

Draw what makes you proud!

I AM PEACEFUL

What wins are you celebrating today?

write or doodle and celebrate YOU

What wins are you celebrating today?
write or doodle and celebrate YOU

I AM

creative

Let's check in!

Take a look at the wins you have written. What do you notice?

_____
_____
_____
_____
_____
_____
_____
_____

Write your affirmations:

I can: _____
I will: _____
I am: _____

Draw what makes you proud!

What wins are you celebrating today?
write or doodle and celebrate YOU

my words are friendly

What wins are you celebrating today?

write or doodle and celebrate YOU

Let's check in!

Take a look at the wins you have written. What do you notice?

_____
_____
_____
_____
_____
_____
_____
_____

Write your affirmations:

I can: _____
I will: _____
I am: _____

ABRACADABRA

Draw what makes you proud!

What wins are you celebrating today?
write or doodle and celebrate YOU

I AM UNIQUE

What wins are you celebrating today?
write or doodle and celebrate YOU

Let's check in!

Take a look at the wins you have written. What do you notice?

_____
_____
_____
_____
_____
_____
_____
_____

Write your affirmations:

I can: _____
I will: _____
I am: _____

Draw what makes you proud!

I AM

POWERFUL

What wins are you celebrating today?
write or doodle and celebrate YOU

MY WORDS ARE MY WAND

ABRACADABRA

What wins are you celebrating today?

write or doodle and celebrate YOU

Let's check in!

Take a look at the wins you have written. What do you notice?

_____
_____
_____
_____
_____
_____
_____
_____

Write your affirmations:

I can: _____

I will: _____

I am: _____

Draw what makes you proud!

What wins are you celebrating today?

write or doodle and celebrate YOU

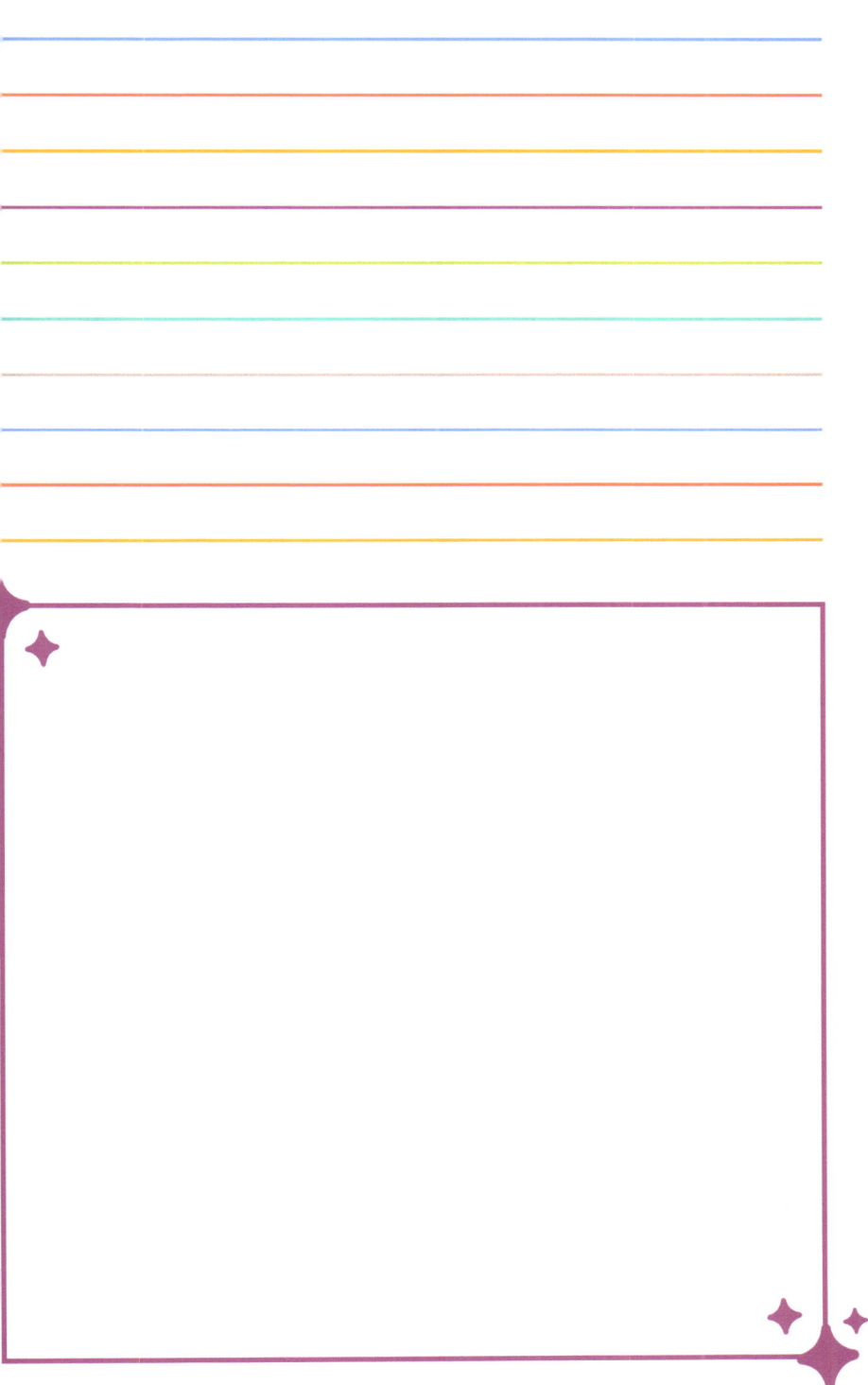

What wins are you celebrating today?
write or doodle and celebrate YOU

Let's check in!

Take a look at the wins you have written. What do you notice?

_____
_____
_____
_____
_____
_____
_____
_____

Write your affirmations:

I can: _____
I will: _____
I am: _____

Draw what makes you proud!

What wins are you celebrating today?
write or doodle and celebrate YOU

my words create possibilities

What wins are you celebrating today?
write or doodle and celebrate YOU

Let's check in!

Take a look at the wins you have written. What do you notice?

_____
_____
_____
_____
_____
_____
_____
_____

Write your affirmations:

I can: _____

I will: _____

I am: _____

ABRACADABRA

Draw what makes you proud!

What wins are you celebrating today?
write or doodle and celebrate YOU

my words create friendships

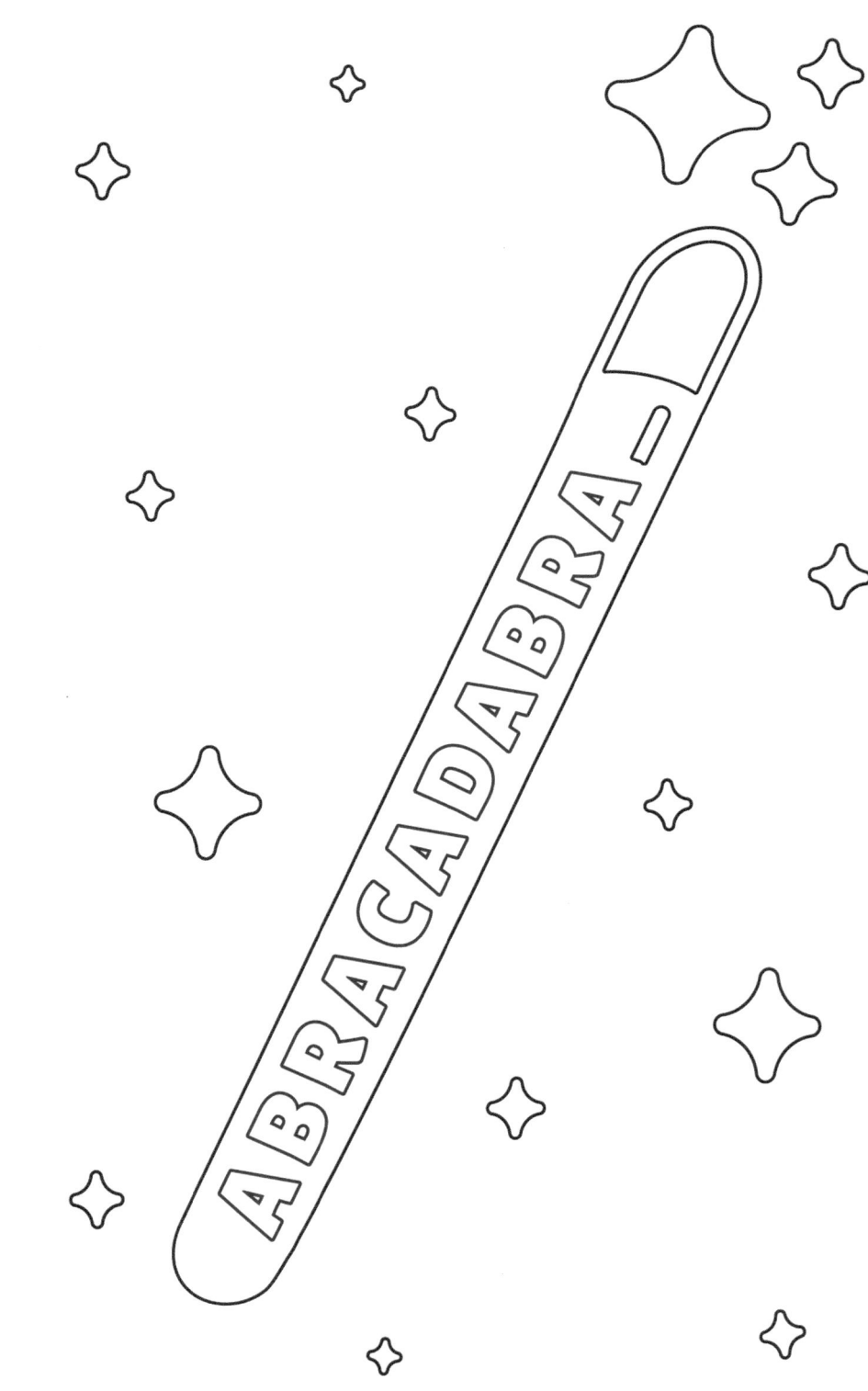

my wins inspire

What wins are you celebrating today?

write or doodle and celebrate YOU

Let's check in!

Take a look at the wins you have written. What do you notice?

_____
_____
_____
_____
_____
_____
_____
_____

Write your affirmations:

I can: _____

I will: _____

I am: _____

ABRACADABRA

Draw what makes you proud!

celebrate YOUR WINS!

Celebrate yourself!
Congratulations! You have filled up this journal with so many wins! Celebrate yourself and keep writing down your wins!

Share your abracadabra moments!

Instagram @languageninjas
Facebook @thelanguageninjas
#abracadabramoment

DISCOVER MORE LEARNING TOOLS

Digital downloads and more are available at
www.languageninjas.me

www.ingramcontent.com/pod-product-compliance
Lightning Source LLC
Chambersburg PA
CBHW040732060526
44119CB00078B/285